"Business for the Beginner – a resource guide to Business ideas and concepts"

This creatively designed handbook is in both English and Chinese and will help those who want to learn and conduct business, understand basic terms and their meanings as well as to help in the advancement of their knowledge in knowing how to do business.

Every day we encounter some kind of a business transaction whether it's going to the supermarket or interacting at work. Understanding how business works and adapting the English meanings can greatly improve one's ability and foresight into improving the bottom line.

Topics that are touched on include HRM (Human Resource Management, Business Accounting (basic explainable math and formulas), Decision making, employee empowerment and many others. Refer to the table of contents)

This short handbook is designed for anyone of any language who wants to get a basic understanding of how business works and tactics that can be used to help you and your company achieve the goals that it wants and to hopefully improve the bottom line.

I have been in China now for 3 years teaching and managing Business classes in Corporations, University and High School. I am well educated and this is my passion and drive – to help others gain insights by using understandable, simple English/Chinese to get a clear cut message about Business.

Table of Contents

Chapter	Title	Page
1	Need and Nature for Business Activity	4
2	Constraints on Business Strategy: Technical, Legal, Social & Environmental	38
3	Marketing issues and concepts	46
4	People in organizations: Motivation and Theory	67
5	Management Roles & Leadership Styles	76
6	Human Resource Management	81
7	Introduction to Operations Management Decisions	87
8	Costs, Break Even Analysis and Costing Methods	92
9	Improving Operational Efficiency: Quality Issues Operational Planning	102
10	Business Accounting and Finance	105

CHAPTER 1

The need and nature for Business Activity

Economic activity and the problem of choice

1. Economic activity:
The purpose of economic activity is to provide for as many of our wants as possible.

The problem of choice:
Because of the shortage of products and the resources needed to make them, all economic units need to make careful and rational choices by choosing those things of the greatest benefit and leaving out those things of less value.

Opportunity cost: The cost of a decision expressed in terms of the lost benefit from the next most desired option. It is the benefit that we are giving up.

What is business activity?
After identifying the needs of consumers or other firms, businesses purchase resources — or factors of production — in order to produce goods and services that satisfy these needs, usually with the aim of making a profit.

Some important business terms:
a) Factors of production:
- Land: land renewable and nonrenewable resources of nature: coal, crude oil, timber
- Labor
- Capital: finance all man-made resources: computers, machines, factories, offices, vehicles
- Enterprise: the driving force, provided by risk-taking individuals that combines the other factors of production into a unit that is capable of producing goods and services. It provides a managing, decision making and coordinating role.

b) Consumer goods:
These are physical and tangible goods sold to the general public.
- Durable goods: car, washing machines;
- Nondurable consumer goods: food, drinks, sweets which can only be used once.

c) Consumer services:
These are non-tangible products that are sold to the general public including hotel accommodation, insurance services and train journeys.

d) Capital goods:
These are physical goods that are used by industry to aid in the production of other goods and services, such as machines and commercial vehicles.

Classification of business activity:
- **Primary sector** is the businesses that operate in industries that are concerned with agriculture, fishing and extraction of raw material.
- **Secondary sector** is made up of industries engaged in manufacturing products or construction.
- **Tertiary sector** is the business activity that provides services for consumers and other businesses.

Industrialization is the term used to describe the growing importance of the secondary sector manufacturing industries in developing countries.

Benefits: GDP and living standards ↑
  exports↑ imports↓
  jobs↑
  tax↑
  adding value↑

Problems: movement of people from county to town → housing and social problems
  import of raw materials and components ↑
  multi-national companies ↑

De-industrialization is the process of a general decline in the importance of secondary sector activity and an increase in the tertiary sector in developed economics.
  Reason: higher income
     Competition

Public and private sectors (legal structure of business organizations)
- ✧ **Private sector**
- ✧ **Public sector**

Private sector is the part of the economy Operated by private individuals or privately owned businesses.

a) Sole traders: An individual owning and operating a business of his /her own.
Small: great in number, but account for only a small proportion of total business turnover

Unlimited liability applies to sole traders and partnerships – these business owners risk losing all personal assets if the venture fails.
Trades: construction, retailing, hairdressing, car- servicing and catering

Partnership: A legal form of business organization in which two or more people – the partners – trade collectively.

Deed of partnership provide agreement on issues such as voting rights, the distribution of profits, the management role of each partner and who has authority to sign contracts.

Limited companies:
- ✧ **Limited liability:** shareholders are only personally liable to lose their original investment in the company in the event of business failure. They cannot be asked to contribute more funds to an insolvent company.
- ✧ **Legal personality:** This is given to companies on incorporation and gives them legal rights and

responsibilities, treating them as separate legal entities in the eyes of the law.
- **Continuity:** death — inheritance of share

Private limited company is an incorporated business that is owned by shareholders but does not have the legal right to offer shares for sale to the public. Often are small, family-owned businesses. Shares are owned by original sole trades (controlling interest), relatives, friends and employees. No new issue share will be sold on open market and shareholders may only sell their share with the agreement of the other shareholders.

Public limited company (PLC / inc) is am incorporated business that has the legal right to offer shares for sale to the public. Shares of these companies are listed on the Stock Exchange.

Stock market: The market for the sale and purchase of public limited company shares and bolds.

→→→→→ Share →→→→→→
↑   ↓
Company   Stock market   public
↑   ↓
←←←←← Funds ←←←←←←

divorce between ownership and control':
Shareholders (ownership)
↓
Annual General Meeting
↓
Board of Directors (control)

Conflict: Shareholders: short-term profits
  Directors: long-term growth

Cooperative:
Agriculture, retailing
features: member share: work, responsibility and decision making
one member one vote share profit equally

advantages: buying in bulk
　　work cooperation

shortages: poor management
　　　capital shortage
　　　slow decision making

Franchise: A business what is based upon the purchase of a franchise license from the franchisor. This allows the name, logo, and products to be used. Franchise businesses have a lower failure rate than non-franchise firms.
Multinational businesses: McDonald's

Joint ventures: The setting up of a business enterprise by two or more firms, often with a specific regional or product responsibility.

Reason:
Share costs and risks
Joints strength and experience
Share market
Risks: different management and culture
Blame each other for mistakes
Business failure

A holding company is one that owns and controls a number of separate businesses, yet does not unite them into one unified company.
Holding company has diversified interests, only has centralized control over crucial issues, such as new investment.
Subsidiary companies are independent to each other.

Legal formalities in setting up a company:
- ✧　　A Memorandum of Association: name, address, maximum share capital, aim
- ✧　　Articles of Association: internal workings and control of the business
- ✧　　The certification of incorporation: Registrar of Company

Public sector enterprises - public corporations
Public sector comprises organizations accountable to and controlled by central or local government (the state). Usually include health and education services, defense, public law, and order (police force).
In some countries, important 'strategic' industries are also stated owned and controlled, such as energy, telecommunications and public transport.
Aim: not profit usually

Privatization is the process of selling state-owned (public sector) businesses to the expected value calculation. School, hospital

Business and economic structure
The function of an economy:
- What? → products
- How? → production
- Who? → customers

Economic system of a country:
- Free market economy:
- Planned economy:
- 'Mixed': free market + government intervention

Market economy (free market economy):
  Key features: private ownership
    Resources are allocated by consumers' needs
    Price determination
    Aim: profit
  Restricted government intervention:
State machine: defense, policy, justice systems
Monetary and financial role: control money supply, inflation, monopoly. Union
  USA, Taiwan

Planned economy:
Features: State ownership and control of resources
   Central planning of production and products distribution;
   Consumers have little influence, and the law of price doesn't work;
Little private business
'Communist' political systems: Cuba, North Korea

Mixed economy: An economic system that combines elements of a free market (private enterprise) and state control and ownership of resources (public sector).
Features: Many products and services: private sectors
Public goods (most essential services, such police, fire service, defense, street lighting, social service and prison: public sectors and private contracting with government
Merit goods (social benefits, such as school, health service, broadcasting): both
Taxes: to finance the state-operated services
Government interventions: control pollution and monopoly

Evaluation of economic systems:
Transforming economics: High tax
   Governmental Control: pollution, labor, location
   Privatization
   Policy: multi-national invest

Nature and scope of international trading links
The great impact of international trade:
Benefits: 1) Products and service imported → more choice
   raw materials: developed economics (import)
      developing countries (industrialization)
   2) Competition → high quality, low price
   3) **Comparative advantage** → economies of scale → cost and price benefits
Countries can specialize in those products that they are best at making if they import those that they are less efficient at from

other countries.
Economies of scale: The factors that lead to reductions in unit cost (average cost) as a firm's scale of operation increases.

INSERT CHART

Drawbacks:
1) competition → loss of output and jobs
2) social, political crisis: strategic goods
3) industrial transformation → job loss and bankrupt
4) **'infant industries'**
5) **'dumping'**
6) import → loss of foreign exchange

Free trade and globalization:
Trade barriers:
- **Tariffs** are taxes imposed on imported goods to make them more expensive.
- **Quotas** are the limits on the physical quantity or value of certain goods that may be imported.
- **Voluntary export limits:** an exporting country agrees to limit the quantity of certain goods sold to one country (possibly to prevent tariffs / quotas being imposed).

Globalization: The trend towards free international trade and free movement of capital between nations. This is resulting in the growth of multinational corporations that seed the widest markets for their uniform products and the cheapest locations for production.

WTO (the World Trade Organization)
Free trade bloc: NAFTA, ASEAN

EU (**European Union**): The union of 15 countries (as at 2002) in Europe that have agreed to act collectively on a wide range of issues rather than nationally.

Multi-national (business) is a business organization that has their headquarters in one country but operating branches, factories and assembly plants in others.

Reasons:
- nearness to markets: lower transport costs for the finished goods: better market information: local advantages and customer loyalty
- lower costs of production: Lower labor rates: Cheaper rent and site cost: Government grants and tax incentives
- avoid import restrictions: no import duties: no import restrictions
- access to local natural resources

Potential problems:

(1) poor communication links
(2) language and culture differences
(3) careful coordination and monitor
(4) training investment

Impact on 'host':
Benefits:
(1) inflow of foreign currency: investment exports
(2) employment↑
(3) local firms: benefit from supplying services or components

Quality and productivity↑
 Management expertise↑
Government tax revenues↑
Nation: GDP↑

Drawbacks:

(1) exploitation: cheap labor, health and safety, poor publicity
(2) pollution:
(3) competition
(4) cultural invasion

(5) profit outflow
(6) depletion of natural resources

Law: Employment Acts:
>Laws passed to regulate contracts of employment, conditions of work and ways in which employees can be dismissed. Some Employment Laws may reduce or define the powers of trade unions.

State intervention:
As layout assistance:
(1) Training programmers
(2) Development area grants:
- Help pay for the building and equipment
- Low rent factories
- Low business tax (free of business tax for a limited period)

(3) Support for exporters:
- Advice service from embassies and government
- Export credit guarantee scheme: ensures payment to firms in case of customer's default, but an insurance premium is payable to the government.

For government intervention:
'laissez-faire' means allowing business to make its own decisions without government intervention.
Disadvantages (the role of government):
- Workforce: low wages, poor conditions, discrimination, no security
- Monopoly: high prices and limited choice

Cartel: An example of restrictive practice or unfair competition that groups producers together in an agreement to restrict output in order to raise or stabilize prices.
When industries are dominated by just a few firms, the could work

together to fix prices and output.
- Consumers' welfare: poor quality, high price, underweighted quantity, no goods safety
- Location: unbalanced development
- Pollution

Against government intervention:
- Business costs
- Administration burden↑
- Unfair competitive advantage

Size of business
- Measurement
- Significance of small businesses
- State intervention to assist and constrain business of different sizes

Different measures of size:
1. Number of employee
   Labor-intensive; in the same industry,
2. Sales turnover:
   In the same industry
3. Capital employed:
   It measures the total value of all long-term finance, in the same industry.

4. Market capitalization = current share price ×total number of shares issued
Public limited company, not stable for the fluctuation of the stock price.

5. Market share = $\frac{\text{Total sale of business}}{\text{Total sales of industry}} \times 100$

6. Others measures:

Hotel: number of guest beds or guest rooms
Retailer: number of shops, total floor sales space

The significance of small businesses:

1. Benefits of small businesses:
- Jobs
- Dynamic entrepreneurs; new ideas; variety → more choices
- Competition
- Growth
- Low costs

2. Problems:
- Lack of specialist management expertise
- Difficulties of raising finance
- Limited product range
- Difficulties in finding suitable and reasonable priced premises

3. Government assistance for small businesses:
- Low tax: reduced rate of profit tax (corporation tax)
- Loan guarantee scheme:
- Drawbacks: higher interest rate
- insurance premium
- Providing information, advice and management support:
- Small Firms Service section of the Department of Trade and Industry
- Finance support: low rent factory

Business objectives and strategy
Objectives and constraints: political, legal, physical, technological, social, environmental, ethical, economic, constraints. Public and private sector business objectives

Hierarchy of objectives:

1. Aim
2. Mission
3. Corporate objectives
4. Divisional objectives
5. Departmental objectives
6. Individual objectives

1. Aims: the long-term goals; customer-based goals
Characteristics: embracing
goal, not strategies
benefits: starting point for the entire set of objectives
help develop a sense of purpose and direction for the whole organization
assessment of the success of business
framework of the strategies

2. Mission: A statement of the business's core aims, phrased in a way to motivate employees and to stimulate interest by outside groups.
Mission statement: A published document that details the agreed common aims of a business so that all managers and staff may work with a shared sense of purpose. Other stakeholders may refer to the mission statement to see what aims the business has.

In favor for:
- quickly inform the central aim to the outside groups;
- Motivation to employees;
- Moral statements or values help to guide the individual employees behavior at work;
- 'what the business is about'

be criticized for:
- too vague and general;
- just for 'feel good';
- impossible to really analyses or disagree;
- rather 'wooly' and general;

3. Corporate objectives: The long-term goals of the corporation that give focus and direction to the business. These form the foundation for the strategic plans of the business.
- **Objectives:** The targets or outcomes that a business attempts to achieve. Overall corporate objectives might include survival, profit, market share and growth – there may be others. Departments will then establish objectives designed to ensure the achievement of the corporate ones.

Common corporate objectives:
(1) Maximizing profits means producing at that level of output where the greatest positive difference between total revenue and total costs is achieved.
Profits → take risks
Limitations:
- The focus on high short-term profits may encourage competitors to enter the market and jeopardize the long-run survival of the business.
- Many business seed to maximize sales in order to secure the greatest market share possible, rather than maximize profits.
- The owners of smaller businesses may be more concerned with leisure time, independence and retaining control.
- Return on capital employed
  - ◆ Job security; environmental concerns
  - ◆ Difficult to assess the point of profit maximization.

(2) Growth: sales, Economies of scale
Limitations:
- ◆ Cash flow problems.
- ◆ Low profit margins
- ◆ Diseconomies of scale
- ◆ Retained profits (using profits to finance growth) leads to lower short-term returns to shareholders
- ◆ Away from 'core' → loss of focus and direction of

the whole business

(3) Increasing market share;
Benefits:
- ✧ Retailers will be keen to stock and promote the best-selling brand
- ✧ Lower profit margins to retailers
- ✧ Brand leader: effective promotional campaigns

(4) Social, ethical and environmental considerations:

(5) Maximizing sales revenue:
- Incentive on managers and staff when salaries and bonuses are dependent on sales revenue.

(6) Maximizing shareholder value:
- Public limited company: increase share prices and returns to shareholders.

(7) Concentrating one core activities:
- Away from huge 'conglomerate' organizations

Main issues:
- bases on the corporate aim
- achievable and measurable
- be communicated to employees and investors
- form the framework of more specific departmental or strategic objectives
- time scale

Determining factors:
(1) Corporate culture is the code of behavior and attitudes that influence the decision-making style of the managers and other employees of the business.
Influencing factors: Small business: personality and management style of owner and leader

Structure of the organization: hierarchical system

Task culture: in some firms the focus is almost solely on 'getting the job done'. The task assumes greater significance than the people doing it.

People culture: people orientated, with great concern for the people doing the job and the extent of their involvement in it. This attitude will bring good productivity because of high team spirit, co-operative spirit and high motivation.

Business culture will determine:
- Objectives of the business
- Way in which the objectives are expressed
- Involvement of the workforce in setting them
- The actions required to achieve objectives are determined and put in effect
- Motivation the workforce show in their efforts towards the achievement of objectives

(2) Size and legal form:
- Small business: satisfying profit
- Larger business: rapid business growth

(3) Public or private sector:
- State-owned organizations: not profit.

(4) Number of years:
- New: survive at all costs
- Once established: pursue other objectives such as growth and profit

Divisional, departmental and individual objectives:
- Set by senior managers to ensure: Co-ordination between all divisions
- Consistency with corporate objectives
- Adequate resources

Management by Objectives (MBO): Once the divisional objectives have been established, then these can be further divided into departmental objectives and targets for individual workers. This process is called MBO.

Establishing strategy:
Four factors:
- Strength of the business
- Resources available
- Competitive environment
- Objectives
-

Stakeholders and their objectives:
Stakeholder: Individuals or groups that have a direct interest in the activities of a business.

1. Shareholders:
Reward:
- after-tax profits
- retained profits for future development
- the prospects for the company and the economy in general are the main driving forces behind share price changes.

Rights:
- receive annual accounts;
- attend the Annual General Meeting to vote
- become a director if elected at AGM
- sell shares on the open market
- limited liability

2. Workforce:
a) Dangers of poor condition: industrial action
- poor productivity
- high absenteeism and labor turnover

- legal intervention
- negative customer reaction

b) Ensure the rights: profitability of the business
- the culture of the organization
- availability of labor supply
- union power
- management attitudes and leadership style

Customers: customer loyalty

Lender – or loan creditors: liquidity; profitability

Community:
Positive: Employment, Spending power
Negative: Traffic, Pollution
Planning authorities have to weigh up the positive and negative effects on the local community.

Government:
Objectives:
- management of economy
- Law
- New laws
- Living standards + environment
- Tax
- Government programs: education, health, road
- Competitive condition

Strategic analysis
Analysis:
- review
- other opportunities (alternative plans)
- risks

SWOT analysis: An assessment of the internal strengths and weaknesses and external opportunities and threats for a business in a given situation. It clarifies issue and problems but it does not take

decision for a business.
S = strengths:
Internal factors (audit): experienced management, loyal workforce and good product range;
W = weaknesses:
Internal factors (audit): poorly trained workforce, limited production capacity, ageing equipment;
O = opportunities:
External audit: Potential areas for expansion: export market, low rates of interest increasing consumer demand
T = threats:
External audit: business and economic environment, market conditions and the strength of the competitors, for example, new competitors, globalization driving down prices, law and policy.

Constraints on business strategies
External economic influences

Economic objectives of government:
'macro-economic' objectives:
- ✧ A target rate of economic growth: GDP
- ✧ A target rate of price inflation
- ✧ Low levels of unemployment
- ✧ A balance between imports and exports (annual Balance of Payments accounts);
- ✧ Exchange rate stability

Economic growth:
Gross Domestic Product (GDP) is the total value of output produced in a country in one year.
Economic growth: an increase in a nation's Gross Domestic 'Product, after adjusting for inflation – an increase in 'real 'GDP. It occurs when the real level of GDP rises as a result of increases in the physical output of goods and services in an economy.

Benefits for nations:
high real GDP → goods and services↑ → living standard↑
output↑ → employment↑ → incomes↑
more resources on public sector
poverty↓
demand↑
tax↑

Benefits for businesses:
1. Production and innovation:
output↑ → employment↑ → incomes↑ → demand↑ → production↑
real GDP↑ → living standard↑ → demand for new products↑ → innovation & technology↑

2. Human resources:
output↑ → profit↑ → motivation to staff↑ → productivity↑
→ more skilled and professional staff

3. Public sector and providers for public sector:
GDP↑ → tax revenue↑ → public sector↑ → demand↑ → production↑

4. Environment and community:
GDP↑ → poverty↓ → crime↓ → better environment and community
output↑ → profit↑ → environment protection↑ → public praise↑

Factors leading to economic growth:
- technology↑ & training↑ → productivity↑ → output↑

Not demand-pull pressures; doesn't lead to inflation;
Governments wish to encourage the growth by encouraging business investment, innovation and staff training schemes.

- total or 'aggregate' demand↑ → Inflation

Business cycle

'Overheated' economy: Inflation can result from demand-pull forces, especially when the economy is nearing full capacity in the later stages of the upswing of the business cycle.

Problems:
Demand-pull inflation↑ → competitiveness↓ → export↓
→ & wage demands↑

Labor shortage↑ → wage↑ → costs↑

House purchase↑ & durable goods↑

Incomes↑ → demands↑ → imports (luxury goods and services)↑
→ export↓   → current-account deficit

Recession: When the real GDP of a country decline – occurs during downturn in the business cycle and is characterized by failing demand for most products.
output↓ → employment↓ unemployment↑ → income↓ → demand↓
→ tax↓

Advantages:
- land property (cheap) investment
- Demand for 'inferior' goods↑
- Relation between employers and employees↑ & efficiency↑
- 'Fitter and leaner'

Inflation and Deflation: changes in the value of money

Inflation: A sustained rise in the average price level. This is measured by the retail price index.

Deflation is a fall in the average price level in an economy - the opposite of inflation. It can also be used to mean a period of declining economic activity.

d) How is inflation measured? The Retail Price Index (RPI): weighted

e) What causes inflation?
Cost-push inflation:
- As the Exchange rate decreases (↓) the price of imported materials increase (↑)
- When world demand increases (↑) prices also increase(↑) →leading to higher costs of production
- As inflation rises so should wages
- Selling prices↑

Demand-pull of inflation
Demand of stock increases and stocks also increase leading to an increase is prices and profit margins decreasing

Impact of inflation on business strategy:
Benefits:
- low-rate inflation

Cost↑ price↑
Real value of debts↓ → borrow↑ → invest↑
Assets (fixed assets, land, building)↑
Stock↑

Drawbacks:

- high-rate inflation (above 10%)

Wage demand↑ → industrial dispute↑
Consumers: price sensitive, economical → bargain > big brand
Interest rate↑
Cash flow problems

Consequence: Inflation↑ → competitiveness in exports↓
Credit sale↓
Consumers stockpile commodities

Businesses in rapid inflation:
Cut investment
Cut profit margin to limit price rises
Reduce borrowing to limit interest
Reconsider credit policy
Reduce labor costs

Deflation:
Damage: Consumers purchases↓
Borrowing to invest↓
Investment↓
Stock↓
The optimum position for most economies is to tolerate low rates of inflation, but to keep a very careful watch to ensure that the rate does not rise above a preset target. (2.5% per annum in UK)

3. Unemployment:

Unemployment exists when members of the working population are willing and able to work, but are unable to find employment.

Cyclical unemployment: Unemployment caused by a downswing in the economic or business cycle. As demand falls during a recession so jobs are lost as businesses reduce output.
Demand↓→ firm's output↓ production↓→ unemployment↑ income↓→ spending↓
↓
Deepening of recession

Structural unemployment: Job losses that occur as a result of significant shifts in the structure of industry, e.g. the decline of coal production or the ending of shipbuilding in a country due to foreign competition. This type of unemployment results in certain types of workers being unable to find work, even though other labor markets are short of labor.

Causes: (1) incomes↑ → change in consumers' tastes and expenditure patterns
(2) Changes in structure of industry
(3) Improvement in technology → adaptable and multi-skilled workers↑
→ jobs losses in declining industries
→ Unemployment of workers who cannot transfer jobs or upgrade skills

Frictional unemployment is the unemployment resulting from the labor market failing to allow a worker to move swiftly from losing one job to finding another. The longer the average period taken for the unemployed to find another job, the greater the level of frictional unemployment.
If labor turnover rates increase in the economy as a whole, then the level of frictional unemployment will increase.

Government policy:
Cyclical:
◇ control economy to avoid substantial swing in business cycle
◇ control inflation, anti-inflationary measures
◇ maintain competitive rate of exchange to protect export

Structural:
◇ education and training programs
◇ training courses to all long-term unemployed

Fictional:
◇ labor market (job centers or employment agencies): more info
◇ reduce unemployment benefits

Costs of unemployment: a waste of human resources
Country:

◇ have to produce more
◇ cost↑ → tax↑
◇ social problems

Businesses:
◇ unemployment↑ → demand↓
◇ frictional unemployment → vacancies → efficiency↓
◇ tax for paying unemployment benefit will fall on business

Unemployed and their families:
◇ income↓ → living standard↓
◇ loss of self-respect
◇ long unemployment → out of date

Balance of payment:
Economic problems caused by a large and persistent deficit on its balance of payments

For country:
- ✧ Exchange rate↓
- ✧ Foreign currency reserves↓
- ✧ Foreign investment↓

For business:
- ✧ Exchange rate problems → import and export risky
- ✧ Government policy (limiting foreign exchange transactions, import control) → retaliation

Exchange Rates:
Exchange rate: The price of one currency in terms of another. It is determined by the forces of supply and demand.

1) Exchange rate fluctuations:
Appreciation: one unit of the currency will buy more units of other currencies. When demand for a currency exceeds supply its value will rise.

Depreciation: The fall in the value of a fixed asset over time. Accountant's record depreciation on accounting statements to give a true picture of an asset's worth and to give a more accurate profit figure than if depreciation was ignored.

2) Appreciation of our currency:
Winners:

(1) Importers of foreign raw materials and components
Currency↑ → domestic currency cost for import goods↓
(imported good cheaper)
→ production cost↓ → competition↑

(2) Importers of foreign manufactured goods
Currency↑ → domestic currency cost for import goods↓
(imported good cheaper) & selling price→ → profit↑

(3) All country
Currency↑ → domestic currency cost for import goods↓
(imported good cheaper) → inflation↓

Losers:

(1) Exports of goods and services to foreign markets:
Currency↑ → foreign currency costs for exported goods↑
(our products in foreign market more expensive)

(2) Business competing foreign competitors in domestic market:
Currency↑ → foreign goods cheaper
→ imported goods↑ domestic goods↓

Depreciation of our currency:
Winners:
Home-based exporters:
Currency↓ → foreign currency costs for exported goods↓
(our products in foreign market cheaper) → exports↑

Businesses face less foreign competition in domestic market:
Currency↓ → foreign goods more expensive → imports↓

Losers:
(1) Manufacturers who depend heavily on imported supplies of material, components or energy sources:
Currency↓ → foreign supply more expensive
→ Production cost↑ → competition↓

(2) Retailers that purchase foreign supplies:
Currency↓ → foreign supply more expensive
→ find domestic supplies

b) International competitiveness: other than price
1) Product design and innovation
2) Quality of construction and reliability
3) Effective promotion and extensive distribution
4) After sale service
5) Investment in trained staff and modern technology

Macro-economic policies:
- Fiscal policy
- Monetary policy
- Exchange rate policy

Fiscal policy:
Fiscal policy is the measures taken by the government to change taxes and the level of government spending. These measures will have an impact on the rest of the economy as they may result in a budget deficit that will expend total demand in the economy. AM increasing government budget surplus will reduce total demand in the economy.
Annual budget: budget deficit / surplus
- Government expenditure: social security, health, education, defense and law and order;
- tax rates: income tax, value added tax, corporation tax ad excise duty;

✧ government borrowing;

Recession: unemployment↑ demand↓
Government policy: expenditure plan↑
Tax↓ → disposable incomes↑ → spending↑ → demand↑

Booming, overheating:
Government policy: expenditure plan↓
Tax↑ → disposable incomes↓ → spending↓ → demand↓

Monetary policy:
Monetary policy: Action taken by the Government or the Central Band to vary the rate of interest or the supply of credit in an economy.
 ✧ Interest rate
 ✧ supply of money

High-inflation: base rate↑
Low-inflation: base rate↓

Booming: Insertion of chart

Government policy and industrial competitiveness:
1. Income tax↓ → motivation↑ → competitiveness↑

2. Corporation tax is a tax on the net profits of limited companies after interest.
Corporation tax↓ → investment↑ → competitiveness↑

3. Interest rate↓ → borrowing cost↓ → competitiveness↑

Exchange rate policy:
¥interest rate↑ → ¥demand for our currency↑ → ¥exchange rate↑

Drawbacks to floating rates (benefits of jointing a common currency):
1) Imported material≈ → production cost≈
2) Export prices≈ → demand≈
3) Profits≈→ risk↑:

1) Import: difficult to compare cost
2) Cost↑: commission cost to bank↑
Price list
Currency 'contracts' and 'hedging': expensive
Dependant on overseas investment
Relocation

Advantages of floating rates (drawbacks of jointing a common currency):
1) Central bank as interest-setting authority
2) Tax policy
3) Interest rate can be adjusted to achieve other economic objectives
4) Conversion costs could be substantial in terms of dual pricing and the changeover of notes

Labor market:
Wage: supply and demand for labor

1. Demand:
a) Costumers' demand↑ → production↑ → demand for labor↑
b) Technology↑ → productivity↑→ demand for unskilled worker↓ →demand for skilled labor↑
Demand for labor of any one type of skill:
- ✧ The demand for the finished products
- ✧ The price and efficiency of labor-saving alternatives, such as machinery

♦ The readiness with which producers increase their capital intensity

2. Supply:
a) Supply of labor to whole economy:
(1) Size of population
(2) Population of working age;
(3) Number of people who choose not to work or who are unable to work;

b) Supply of labor to an industry:
(1) Wage rate;
(2) Availability of suitable labor in other industry;
(3) Unemployment;

c) Supply of labor to an individual business:
(1) Wage;
(2) Availability of suitable labor in other firms;

3. Skill shortages and surpluses:
Skill shortages arise when the demand from industry for a particular type of worker is not matched by the supply of suitably qualified staff.
a) Solutions of a business:
(1) Higher wages to attract new staff:
Advantages: quick
New ideas and experiences
Disadvantages: more expensive than training own workers;
New staff: induction training
Old staff: demand wage rise
(2) Train own staff:
Advantages: no induction training
Disadvantages: Time consuming
Outflow of qualified staff

4. Government intervention:
a) Minimum wage legislation:
(1) Supports: trade union argues that it has brought benefits without causing serious economic disadvantages.

(2) Against: wage↑ → price↑ → inflation
→ competition↓
More wage claim

b) EU Working Time Directive: more staff
more efficient methods of working

Market failure:
Market failure occurs when free markets fail to allocate resources in an effective way or when market prices fail to reflect the full cost to society of production, e.g. pollution.

a) External costs:
External costs are costs of an economic activity that are not directly paid for by the consumer or the producer. These costs have to be borne by society and include pollution from industrial processes and the costs associated with traffic congestion. They are an example of market failure and governments may use cost-benefit analysis to attempt to establish the value of these costs when a major project if planned.
Government: business to take action
Fines and limits
tax

b) Labor training:
The country has a shortage of skilled workers and professional staff
→ economic growth↓
Government: levy members to pay for industry-wide training
Tax → college fund

c) Monopoly producers:
Monopoly: A firm that dominates a market – in theory a single producer within a market. Most countries have, for policy purposes, a wider definition such as 'a firm with at least 25% market share' (UK)
restrict output
prices↑　　　　→ high profit
prevent competitors
Government: purchase from other suppliers

Competition policies

Chapter 2

Constraints on Business Strategies Technological, Legal, Social and Environmental Influences

Technology: impacts
1. Communication:
Internet: much work is done by computer;
the interface with suppliers and customers is largely through computer
problems: isolation
 computer stress
2. Product technology:
CAD CAM: It determines the nature and speed of production flow on the line, the quality of the product, the part that workers play in the process and the creation or disposal of waste.
New products emerge and new demands are created such as computer games.
3. Costs of production:
Technology → fixed cost↑ → large market to spread fixed costs and reduce unit costs →Merging
↓
Large capital, market share and capital intensity
employees↓   → labor productivity↑ → unit cost↓ }
↓
Big firm
4. Human resources:
Redundancies
Employment↑ in technology related industries
Deskilling: reorientation of skills
Multi-skilling
Change attitudes
Small business ← redundancy
Flattening of organization charts
Shortage of skilled computer engineers and programmers
Increasing acceptance of change
5. Marketing:
New products
Buying way: 'shop from home through the Internet or television'.

Pricing:
Ability to compete
Pattern of demand
Distribution
Holiday, leisure goods and entertainment service ← higher disposable incomes
Paying way: credit or debit cards
Fitness-&leisure-based products and services ← more leisure time
Health and medicine: life-saving drugs and operation

Negative effects:
1. Need for data protection:
2. Need for computer use protection:
3. Cost
4. Need for reliability
5. Human relations
6. Health
7. Employment
8. Management
9. Investment
10. Technological literacy

Law:
The employee is personally responsible, but the prime responsibility lies with the employers, who, sensibly, should insure against such risks.

1. Employment practices:
a) Recruitment employment contracts and termination of employment
- A written contract of employment
- Minimum ages
- Maximum working week
- Holiday and pension entitlements
- Discrimination
- Paternity leave
- Termination of employment: large-scale redundancies –

where many workers have their contracts of employment ended- have to be discussed with trade union leaders and with works councils before the courts will accept the legality of the action.
- ✧ Unfair dismissal: pregnancy

Refusal to work on a holy day
Refusal to work overtime if total working hours over forty-eight hours in one week
Incorrect dismissal procedure
Being a member of a trade union

b) Health and safety at work
- ✧ To protect workers from discomfort and physical injury at work.
- ✧ Safety equipment
- ✧ Washing and toilet facilities
- ✧ Protection from dangerous machinery and materials
- ✧ Adequate breaks and working temperatures

c) Impacts on business:
- ✧ Business costs↑ →: Supervisory costs↑
- ✧ Minimum wage↑ → wage costs↑
- ✧ Paid holiday, pension, maternity and paternity leave↑ → costs↑
- ✧ More staff to avoid over-long hours
- ✧ Protective clothing and equipment

d) Benefits:
- ✧ workers: more secure and satisfied
- ✧ reduce risks of accidents and tome off work for ill health or injury
- ✧ attract best employees
- ✧ business culture

Consumer rights:
a) why?
1) To protect the relatively weak individual consumers

2) It is difficult for consumers to understand more scientific products
3) Selling techniques
4) imported goods which adopt different quality and safety standards
5) Competition and monopoly: reduce quality, service, guarantee periods
UK law: Sales of Goods Acts   Trade Descriptions Act   Consumer Protection Act

b) Impact of consumer protection laws on business:
1) business cost↑
2) Redesigning products
3) quality and quantity control → legal action↓
4) Putting consumer interests at the forefront of company policy
5) Public relationship

Business competition:
a) Competition
1) Benefits of competition: wider choices
Low prices
Better quality
Compete with foreign firms to strengthen the domestic economy
2) Competition law: control monopolies and prevent mergers
Limit or outlaw uncompetitive practices
3) The Competition Commission

b) Monopoly:
1) How?
- Patents
- Merging or taking over
- Legal protection
- 'barrier to entry': technology, huge investment
- Privatization of state monopolies: telecommunications and energy

2) Consumers affected:
Benefits: lower prices ← large-scale production(economics of scale)
New products and technical advances

drawbacks: higher prices ← little competition
Limited choice of products
Less investment in new products
No incentive to lower costs and improve efficiency

3) Uncompetitive or restrictive practices:
- Refusal to supply retailer
- Full line forcing; when a major producer forces a retailer to stock the whole range of products from the manufacturer- not just the really popular ones.
- Marking sharing agreements: **Cartel**
- **Predatory pricing:** when a major firm in an industry tries to stop new competitors joining it by charging very low prices for certain goods. If the new firm were to fail, the big firm could then raise its prices once more.

C: Social influences:
1. An ageing population:
2. Role of woman:
3. education↑ → students for part-time job↑
4. early retirements & higher pensions → leisure↑
5. divorce rates↑ → single person households↑
6. job insecurity↑ → temporary and part-time job↑

1. An ageing population:
A larger proportion of population over age of retirement;
A small proportion of the population in lower age ranges (0-16)
Lower birth rate: smaller family, birth control, longer life expectancy
Burdens on the health service, pensions, private pension funds and care industries
Impact on business: changing patterns of demand
Age structure of the workforce

2. Patterns of employment:
a) capital intensive → productivity↑ → total employment↓
b) old industries → new hi-tech industries
c) woman↑: Full-time job

d) Student employment
e) Flexible hours
f) Multi-cultural
g) limited working time

3. Effects:
Higher-quality workers → efficiency↑ salary↑
Part-time job: flexible, training
Woman↑: Removing barriers to the promotion
Cost↑← maternity leave and

D: Environment:
1. Corporate responsibility
When a firm does accept their legal and moral obligations to stakeholders other than investors it is said to be accepting **'corporate responsibility'**.
Ethics are the moral guidelines that determine decision making.
For:
    a) 'green' equipment or use recycled material → marketing and promotional advantage
    b) Low-polluting production methods and responsible waste disposal → lawsuit and fine↓
    c) Environmentally friendly strategy attract potential employees
    d) Long-term financial benefits and reduce the 'external costs': solar energy

Against:
    a) Cheaper goods
    b)   Profits↓
    c) Weak legal protection
    d)   Economic development is more important than environment protection

Pressure groups:
Pressure group is an organization formed by people who share the same objective and attempt to influence business or government decisions in order to achieve them, e.g. Greenpeace.

Greenpeace; Worldwide Fund for Nature; Amnesty International; Jubilee 2000

Aims: a) governments to change their policies and to pass laws supporting the aims of the group;

b) Businesses to change policies to cause less damage to environment;

c) Consumers to change their purchasing habits to push business to adopt 'appropriate' policies

Ways: a) Media coverage: effective public relations

b) Influencing consumer behavior

c) Lobbying of government

Environmental audits:

Audit is an independent check on the accuracy of a firm's accounting process and the fairness of the final accounting statements. It is designed to give shareholders confidence in the fairness and accuracy of the final accounts.

Pollution levels, wastage levels and recycling rates of the business and compare them with previous years and pre-set targets.

Good audits reports → Favorable consumer reaction → sales↑

Environmental audit is an independent check aiming to assess the degree to which a company is fulfilling its social responsibilities – especially towards the environment. It includes data such as pollution levels and usage rate of non-renewable resources.

The Internet

Business opportunities/threats; e-commerce, e-business

Increase use of the internet for consumer goods is allowing consumers to choose form a wider range of suppliers and this will bread down some monopoly situations.

Stakeholders

Owners, employees, customers, suppliers, community, government bodies

Corporate culture and strategy

Organization behavior, method of operation

CHAPTER 3

Marketing Decision
Marketing Issue and Concepts

A: Marketing:

A Market means any place where buyers and sellers meet to arrange a sale/purchase, 'who the consumers are'

Marketing is the process of researching into and identifying consumer needs and employing appropriate price, product, place and promotion strategies in order to satisfy these needs profitably.

1. Market orientation and product orientation:
a) Market orientation

Market orientation is a business strategy focusing on the needs and wants of consumers and developing products to meet them. This approach requires market research and market analysis to indicate present and future consumer demand.
Consumer first

Benefits:
Effective market research → reduce the failing of new products

Survive longer and higher profit

Constant feedback

b) Product orientation:

technical innovation → new products → needs↑

High-quality product

c) Asset-led marketing:

This is based on market research too but does not attempt to satisfy all consumers in all markets. The firm will consider its own strengths in terms of people, assets and image and will only make those products that use and take advantage of strengths.

2. Marketing process:

1) Establishing marketing objectives
2) Carrying out effective market research and identifying target groups
3) Analyzing the markets the firm operates in or plans to enter
4) Designing and developing the product
5) Testing consumer reaction to product, price and packaging
6) Deciding on the most appropriate price
7) Establishing a suitable promotion strategy and promotion budget
8) Effective distribution system

Distribution channels: The routes taken by products or services from producer to consumers.

9) Assessing products sales against target- adjusting marketing variables if sales fail to meet budgeted levels

a) Marketing objectives:
Marketing objective: the objectives that the marketing department will pursue in order to meet the objectives of the whole business, e.g. market leadership.

1) Fit in with the overall aims and mission of the business;
2) Be determined by senior management
3) Be realistic, motivating, achievable, measurable and clearly communicated to all

the organization

b) Cooperation with other departments:
Production; Human resources; Finance

c) Achievements:
Market share
Sales target: number of units or sales revenue
Market penetration: increasing sales in existing markets
Market development: selling existing products or introducing innovation ones to new markets

d) Importance:
Direction
Assessment and corrective action
Short-term targets
Cooperation with other departments'
Starting point of marketing strategy

B: Market segmentation:
A **Market segment** is a sub-group of a whole market in which consumers have similar characteristics., e.g. age, sex, income, region. Identifying these different groups and marketing different products or services to them is called **market segmentation**.

1. Niche marketing:
Market niche: An unexploited gap that exists within a market for goods or services.
Niche marketing is the business strategy of devising and selling products specifically for a small unexploited part of a market. Although lacking benefits such as economies of scale, small producers are often able to survive by adopting this strategy even though the rest of the market is dominated by much larger firm.
Advantages: small market survives in a segment
High prices and high profit margins
Large firms create status and image

2. Mass marketing
Mass marketing involves selling the same products to the whole

market with no attempt to target groups within it.
Advantages: economies of scale
Fewer risks

C: Market share, market size, market growth
1. Market share: The percentage of total market sales held by one brand or business.

<u>Sales for this business</u> ×100
Total market sales
Brand leader is the product with the highest market share.

Benefits of a high market share:
High sales
Retailers: willing to stock and promote
prominent position in shops
better discount rate

2. Market growth is the percentage increase in the size of the whole market.
Measurement: volume: number of units sold
Value: sales revenue

3. Adding value means the difference between the selling price of a product and the cost of the materials and components bought in to make it.

Added value↑ → profit↑
  a) Create an exclusive and luxurious retail environment to make consumers feel that they are being treated as important;
  b) Use high-quality packaging to differentiate the product from other brands;
  c) Promote and brand the product: brand name
  d) Create a USP 'unique selling point' that clearly differentiate a product form that of other manufacturers.

Unique selling point (USP): The distinctive feature of a product or service that a business will use to differentiate it from rivals.。

4. Market segmentation:
a) Geographic differences:
b) Demographic differences:
age, sex, family size and ethnic background
c) Psychographic factors:
1) Social class (income) → expenditure patterns
6 socio-economic groups:
A: Higher managerial, administrative and professional
B: Middle managerial
C1: Supervisory, clerical or junior managerial
C2: skilled manual workers
D: Semi and unskilled manual
E: Casual, part time workers and unemployed

2) Lifestyles: activities undertaken, interests and opinions

3) Personality characteristics

Market research and sales forecasting

Market research is the process of collecting and analyzing data relating to demand for a goods or service in a specific market such as market size and trends, competitors, consumer buying habits and likely sales levels.

Consumer's reactions to:
different price levels
Alternative forms of promotion
Packaging
Distribution

Need for market research:
- ✦ Reduce the risk of new product
- ✦ Predict future changes
- ✦ Explain patterns in sales of existing products and market trends
- ✦ To assess the most favorable designs, flavors, styles, promotions and packages for a product.

Information:
- ✦ market size
- ✦ consumer tastes and trends
- ✦ products: strength and weakness
- ✦ promotion
- ✦ competitors
- ✦ distributions
- ✦ packaging

A: Primary and secondary research:

Primary research: The gathering of original first-hand data from people within your target market.

Secondary data: Data that are used even though they are originally collected for another purpose, e.g. government statistics.

Sources of secondary data:
- ✦ Government publications:

Social trends
Economic trends
Annual abstract of Statistics
Family Expenditure Survey
- ✦ Local libraries and local population census

Local government offices
- ✦ Trade organizations

- Market Intelligence Reports
- Newspaper reports and specialist publications
- Internal company records

Customer sales records
Guarantee claims
Daily, weekly and monthly sales trends
Feedback from customers on product, service, delivery and quality

1. Methods of primary research:
a) Qualitative research technique:
Qualitative research: Market research that focuses on the consumer motivations that explain consumer buying behavior. For example, it does not focus on 'how much will be bought' but 'why consumer choose to buy one product rather than another'.

Technique: interviews with individual consumers or groups of them.

In-depth discussions ←psychologists to identify key factors influencing consumer choice

b) Quantitative research technique:
Quantitative research: Collection of research data in a numerate form.

1) Observation: observe and record how consumers behave
2) **Test marketing**: Before a full-scale launch, produce a limited quantity of a new product. It involves promoting and selling the product in a limited geographical area and recording consumer reactions and sales figures.
3) Consumer survey: directly ask consumers or potential consumers for the opinions and preferences.

Who to ask?
Sample size:

Larger the sample, the more confidence
Cost and time
Sampling methods:
Random sample: When every person in the population being surveyed has an equal chance of being selected

Stratified sample: The selection of a research sample that draws respondents from a limited and specific section of that population, e.g. all people over the age of 65 years for research into demand for retirement homes.

Quota sample: When the demographic profile of the population is known and samples are drawn from it in proportion to the characteristics of the population, e.g. if 60% of consumers of soft drinks are between 18-25 then 60% of the sample should be chosen form this age range.

Cluster sample: When product is mainly to appeal to specified groups of consumers, for example town or regional newspapers.
What to ask?
Questionnaire design
How to ask?
Self-completed questionnaire or direct interview
How accurate is it?
Sampling bias: Results from a sample may be different from those that would have been obtained if the entire target population had been questioned.
Questionnaire bias: when questions tend to lead respondents towards one particular answer.
Other bias: respondent not answering in a very truthful way.
2. Market research developments:
Presentation of data:
Bar charts; Histograms; Line graphs; Pie charts

The marketing mix - product

Marketing mix: The variables that can be adjusted by managers to achieve a marketing strategy – **'4P'** product, price, promotion and place (distribution).

Market position: Placing the product within a market in terms of image, pricing, target consumer and so on.

NPD: New product development

The **Brand** is the distinguishing name or symbol that is used to differentiate one manufacturer's products from another.

Before deciding on which product to develop and launch, it is common for firms to analyze how the new brand will relate to the other brands in the market. This is called **positioning** the product by using a technique such as market mapping.

Market mapping: Analyzing the main rivals in a market by using a two-dimensional grid with two key variables, e.g. price and product image.

A: new product development:
1. Process of new product development:
- ✦ Research and development
- ✦ Product testing
- ✦ Market testing

2. Research and development:
a) R&D (research and development): risky

- ➤ **'Offensive':** An offensive R&D strategy will be to lead the rest of the industry with innovations products to gain market share and, possibly, market dominance.
- ➤ **'Defensive':** A defensive strategy will be to attempt to learn from the initial innovators' mistake and weaknesses. It aims to improve on the original products or develop slightly different types of goods which might appeal to other market segments.
- ➤ **"NO R&D":** license other businesses' new ideas or adapt existing products into 'me too' look-alikes.

Safer → legal battles of copy right

b) Government encouragement:
- ✧ **'Patent'** or **'register'**: legal security to inventors and designers
- ✧ Financial assistance

3. Screening process:
Stage: Idea screening→concept testing→product development → test marketing → national launch
It is designed to reduce the risk to minimum.

4. factors influencing expenditure of R&D
The nature of product
The R&D spending plans of competitors
Business expectations
The risk profile or culture of the business
Government policy

5. Evaluation:
Reasons to failure:
Inadequate market research
Poor marketing support or inappropriate pricing
Changes in technology leave the product dated
Competitors' better product

B: Product life cycle: The stages through which all products that survive their initial launch will pass before being withdrawn from the market at the end of their commercial life.

a) Stages:
1) Introduction:
2) Growth:
3) Maturity or saturation:

Market saturation: A stage that all markets can reach when most consumers already own the product, e.g. televisions, and most sales are therefore replacement sales. The market has

stopped growing.
4) Extension:
Such strategies include developing new markets for existing products, for example export markets, new uses for existing products and re-launches involving new packaging and advertising.
5) Decline

b) 3 Usages:
1) Assisting with the planning of marketing mix decision

2) Identifying how cash flow might depend on the cycle

Development stage: cash flow is negative
Growth: sales↑ → cash flow↑
Maturity or saturation: high sales, low promotion costs → cash flow↑
Decline: price↓ sales↓ → cash flow↓
3) Recognizing the need for a balanced product portfolio

A balanced product portfolio is meant that factory capacity should be kept at roughly constant levels as declining output of some goods is replaced by increasing demand for the recently introduced products.

The marketing mix – pricing decisions
A: Demand and consumer behavior:
1. Price: 'demand curve'
Income effect: price↑ → spending power↓ → demand↓
Substitution effect: When one product's price rises it seems more expensive compared to other, similar, goods. Many consumers will now buy substitutes instead.

2. Non-price factors:
   1)   wage↑ → incomes↑
   2)   interest rates↓ → demand↑
   3)   population↑ → demand for target goods↑

4) prices of substitute goods↑ → demand↑
price of complementary goods↓ → demand↑
5) effective advertising and promotion

B: Price elasticity of demand is the relationship between price changes and the size of the resulting change in demand.

PED = <u>Percentage change in quantity demanded</u>
       Percentage change in price

1. Factors that determine PED:
a) How necessary the product is.
More necessary, less elastic
b) How many similar competing products or brands there are.
More competitors, more substitutes, more elastic
c) The degree of consumer loyalty
Higher the consumer loyalty, less reaction
Product differentiation: all businesses attempt to increase brand loyalty with influential advertising and promotional campaigns and by making their products more distinct.
d) The price of product:
Cheaper, lower elastic

2. Uses: a) Accurate sales forecasts
b) Pricing decision

C: The pricing decision:
1. Costs of production: fixed costs + variable cost
2. Competitive conditions
3. Competitors' prices
4. Business and marketing objectives
5. PED
6. Whether it is a new or an existing product
 'Skimming' or 'penetration'

D: Pricing methods:
1. Cost-based pricing: firms assess the costs per unit and add an amount on top of the calculated cost.
a) Mark-up pricing:
Retailers: buying costs + mark up (demand, other suppliers, life

stage of product)
b) Target pricing:
A required rate of return at a certain level of output/sales

c) Full cost (absorption cost) pricing:
Unit cost + profit margin
d) Contribution cost (marginal cost):
Unit variable cost + contribution to fixed cost

2. Competition-based pricing:
a) **Price leadership**
b) **Similar prices** to avoid a price war
c) **Destroyer pricing**: low prices to force competitors out of the market
d) **Market pricing** (consumer-based pricing):
1) Perceived value pricing (customer value pricing): inelastic, real value
2) **Price discrimination**: Firms can price discriminate if there are different groups of consumers, with different elasticities of demand for the product, and where the firm is able to avoid resale between the groups.

3) New product pricing:
- **Penetration pricing** is a relatively **low price** is set and strong promotion takes place in order to achieve a high volume of sales. Aim: to use mass marketing and gain a large market share.
- **Skimming** occurs when a firm has a **unique produc**t that competitors will copy so it attempts to make relatively **high short-term profits** by charging a high price for as long as the product can hold its strong position.

3. Pricing decision –additional issues:
a) Different types of markets:
1) competitor- based pricing: Perfect competition
2) Monopoly:
3) Oligopoly: price wars to gain market share
  Non-price competition
Collusion
  b) Loss leaders:
  1) Retailer: low prices for some products – possibly below variable costs – in the expectation that consumers will buy other goods too.
  2) Firms: encourage purchase of closely related complementary goods: cheep razors：razor/blades
c) Psychological pricing: The strategy of pricing a product in accordance with the value that consumers attach to the good.
1) Manufacturers and retailers set prices just below key price levels in order to make the price appear much lower that it is.
2) The use of market research to avoid setting prices that consumers consider to be inappropriate for the style and quality of the product.

E: pricing decisions – an evaluation:
It is important to apply different methods to its portfolio of products, depending on costs of production and competitive conditions within the market.
Price：Different price levels on potential demand
Brand image or 'life style'
A low price for a prestige 'lifestyle' product could easily destroy the image that the rest of the marketing mix is attempting to establish.

Marketing decisions: promotion and place

Promotion: is about communication with actual or potential customers.
Advertising
Direct selling
Sales promotion offers

A: Promotion objectives:
1. Consumer awareness
2. Remind consumers'
3. Increase purchases and attract new consumers'
4. Demonstrate products
5. Create or reinforce the brand image
6. Correct misleading reports
7. Public image

B: Promotion decisions:
1. Above-the-line promotion:
Media (radio, TV and newspaper)
a) Advertisements:
Informative advertising: Paid for means of communication with the market to give consumers factual information (price, technical specifications or main features and place) rather tan to create a product image;
Persuasive advertising is used to distinguish those advertisements that concentrate only on creating an image of a product rather than giving consumers information.
b) Advertising agencies:
Market research 市场调查
Most cost-effective forms of media
Creative designs
Film or print
Monitor and feedback

2. Below-the-line promotion: all forms of promotion
Below the line is the promotion what is not undertaken by paid-for advertising — such as special offers, sales promotions and inducements to purchase, point-of-sale displays and public relations.
a) 'Money off' coupons and other consumer incentives

Sales promotion can have a very significant short-term effect on sales, but, after the promotion is over, sales often fall back to former levels – or even below, if the promotion has encouraged

multiple purchases that will take some time to be consumed.
b) Direct mail shots to people identified by market research to have a potential interest in product
c) Point of sale displays: best position in retail shops, eye-catching displays, 'brand leader'
d) Sponsorship of sports or cultural events
e) Loyalty cards

3. Promotion mix

4. Branding:
Benefits: Increase the chances of consumer recall
Clearly differentiate the product from others
Allow for the establishment of a 'family' of closely associated products with the same brand
Brands-loyalty → price elasticity↓
Brand loyalty exists when consumers purchase the same product time after time — even though rival products may exist.

5. Advertising expenditure and the trade cycle:
Firms tend to spend more in economy booming than in recession.

C: Promotion budget:
Total spending & how the budget is allocated between the competing forms of promotion.
1. Society and consumer: waste of resources
2. Business:
Assessment: Sales performance
Consumer awareness data
Consumer panels: qualitative feedback
Response rates to advertisements

D: Media:
   Cost
      Size of audience
      The profile of the audience in terms of age, income levels, interests and so on
      The message to be communicated

The other aspects of the marketing mix
The law and other constraints

E: Public relations: deal with the media such as the press and TV companies to obtain favorable reports about the business and its products.

PR departments try to arrange as much **positive** press and TV coverage of their business and products as possible (such as press conference for a launch of a new product or some benefits and incentives offered to the journalists) and take quick and effective response to the **negative** incidents and reports which might damage seriously the reputation of business.

F: Industrial goods:
Specialist magazines or journals
Trade promotion will be used instead of consumer sales promotions
Financial support to aid buyers with the purchase of expensive equipment

G: Packaging:
Functions:
- Protect and contain the product
- Give information, depending on the product, to consumers about contents, ingredients, cooking instructions, assembly instructions and so on
- Support the image of the product created by other aspects of promotion
- Aid the recognition of the product by the consumer

Cheap and nasty packaging of goods will destroy any quality and status image that the firm was attempting to establish.

Distinctive packaging can help to form the basis of a promotional theme which will endure long.

Expensive and wasteful packaging may add unnecessarily to costs that could reduce a product's competitiveness and will increase environmental pressures, and may incite a negative consumer reaction.

Therefore, the use of recycled and recyclable materials in packaging is increasing.

H: Promotion and product life cycle:

I: Place decision:
1. Direct route (direct marketing):
Advantage: cut profit margin of intermediaries or 'middleman'
Full control of pricing and marketing
Efficiency
  Disadvantage: Stocks
Distance and after-sale service
'Junk mail'
2. Retailer
Advantage: Stock of retailer
Concentrate on manufacturing
Disadvantage: profit margin for retailers
Decisions on marketing policy are under control of retailers

3. Factors influencing choice of distribution channel:
a) Industrial products: direct
b) Geographical dispersion
c) Internet
d) Manufacturer wishes to keep complete control: direct

e) Bulk buying: direct

Marketing strategy and market planning
A: Key determinants:
1. Resource limits
2. Business marketing objectives
3. Channels
4. Competitors' actions
5. Market conditions
6. Non-financial resources: staffing

B: The marketing plan:

1. Where are we now?
SWOP analysis
2. What are we aiming for? – Marketing objectives

3. Alternative marketing strategies – making the choice

Market skimming VS Market penetration
Market development involves selling existing products to new consumers in new markets.
Product development is adapting and updating the existing product to maintain consumer interest or developing brand new ones.
4. Planning the implementation of the strategy:
Communication between different departments: finance, production, human resources
Review and revise
5. How successful was it? – reviewing the outcome

C: the market budget: Sales targets Finance

Approaches of marketing expenditure budget:
1. A percentage of sales: sales↑ → funds↑
2. Objective-based budgeting: target sales → expenditure
3. Competitor-based budget:
4. What can we afford?
5. Incremental budgeting: last year budget + percentage

- Low absenteeism
- Low labor turnover

Indicators of poor staff motivation:
- Absenteeism: is the deliberate absence for which there is not a satisfactory explanation.
- Lateness
- Poor performance: poor quality work; low levels of work or greater waste of materials;
- Accidents: careless
- Labor turnover: is leave of staff for reasons that are not positive.
- Grievances: → union disputes

F.W. Taylor and scientific management:
Technique: establishing an idea or a hypothesis, studying and recording performance at work, altering working methods and re-recording performance;
Detailed recording and analysis of results:
Aim: reduce the level of inefficiency that exited in the US manufacturing industry.
Any productivity gains could be shared between business owners and workers.

Taylor's scientific approach: how to improve productivity
1) Select worker
2) Observe performing
3) Record time
4) Quickest method
5) Train supervise
6) Pay on basis results

'Economic man': man was driven or motivated by money alone and the only factor that could stimulate further effort was the chance to earning extra money.

Taylor's motivational suggestion: **wage levels based on output,' piece rate'**

Result: mass production & flow line techniques, specialization

Workers specializing in one task, strict management control over work methods and payment by output level were important features of successful production line techniques.

Taylor's approach and modern advancement:
- Economic man: money + a wide range of needs
- Select the right people for each job
- Observe and record the performance: 'time and motion study' + co-operation and involvement of staff
- Method study: worker participation
- Piece work payment:

2. Elton Mayo and the human relations theories:
a) **'Hawthorne Effect'**: Workers respond positively to human relations approach from managers that focus on taking an active interest in staff and allowing them to operate in groups.

- ✓ Working conditions in themselves were not that important in determining productivity level;
- ✓ Other motivational factors

b) Conclusion:
- ✓ Working condition and financial reward have little or no effect
- ✓ Consultation and interest with workers
- ✓ Team spirit
- ✓ Self-control and self-decision
- ✓ Groups
- ✓ 'people'
- ✓ Participation: giving workers more of a role in business decision making

✓ Involving workers, taking an interest in their welfare and finding out their individual goals

3. Maslow and the hierarchy of human needs:

Hierarchy of needs: Maslow's view that human needs can be presented in the form of a pyramid or hierarchy with lower level needs – such as physical and social needs – and higher order needs – such as esteem and self actualization.

- Self- actualization: challenging work, new skills
- Esteem: recognition for work done well
- Social: working in teams or groups, good communication
- Safety: contract of employment, job security, health and safety conditions
- Physical needs: income

If work can be organized so that we can satisfy some or all of our needs at work then we will become more productive and satisfied.

4. Herzberg and the 'Two factor theory':

Herzberg's research was based around questionnaire and interviews with employees with the intention of discovering.

a) Conclusion:

'Motivators': Job satisfaction resulted form 5 factors

    Achievement
    recognition for achievement
    work itself
    responsibility
    advancement

'Hygiene factors': Job dissatisfaction resulted from 5 factors
Company policy and administration
Supervision

Salary
Relationships with others
Working conditions

Hygiene factors: are extrinsic to the job and can cause dissatisfaction if they are not adequately provided including salary, work conditions and excessive supervision.

> ➢ Extrinsic factors: factors surrounding the job
> ➢ Intrinsic factors: work

b) Consequences:
1) pay and working conditions↑ → remove dissatisfaction, but will not provide condition for motivation to exist
Movement: It was possible to encourage someone to do job by paying them but it does not mean that someone wants to do the job.
Pay moves people to do a job but not motivate them to do it.
   3) The motivators need to be in place for workers to be prepared to work willingly and to always give of their best.

'If you want people motivated to do a good job, give them a good job to do.'
'job enrichment'
Complete units of work
Feedback on performance: recognition for work well done → incentives to achieve more
A range of tasks: challenge; 'self-actualization'
3) A business could offer higher pay, improved working conditions and less heavy-handed supervision of work → remove dissatisfaction

c) Evaluation:
   ✓ Team working
   ✓ Two-way communication

Motivation in practice
A: Payment or financial reward systems:
   1. **Hourly wage rates**: weekly
manual, clerical and 'non-management':
   2. **Price rate**:
The piece rate can be adjusted to reflect the difficulty of the job and the 'standard' time needed to complete it.
   3. **Salary**:
An annual sum usually paid monthly
Professional, supervisory and management staff
Status and post
Job evaluation
   4. **Commission**: personal selling
Base salary + commission
 security↓challenging
   5. **Performance-related pay (PRP)**:
Above-average work performance;
Management, supervisory and clerical posts
Procedure: target → annual appraisals → bonus
Power of senior managers → favoritism

Profit sharing:
The staff will feel more committed to the success of the business and will strive to achieve higher performances and cost savings.
   6. **Fringe benefits**:
Non-monetary reward: company cars, free insurance and pension schemes, private health insurance, discounts on company products and low interest rate loans;
Give status to higher-level employees and to recruit and retain the best staff

B: Non-financial motivation:
1. **Job rotation**: Increasing the flexibility of the workforce and the variety of the work they do by moving them from job to job to relieve the boredom and encourage multi-skill.

2. **Job enlargement**: increase the scope of a job by broadening or deepening the tasks undertaken, so that it is more complete or more challenging;

Job rotation + job enrichment

3. **Job enrichment**: Based on the work of Herzberg, this aims to use the full capabilities of workers so that they are given an opportunity to be more fulfilled at work. Jobs are made more challenging, workers made more accountable and greater feedback on performance is provided.
   - ✓ Complete unit of work → challenge↑
   - ✓ Direct feedback → progress↑
   - ✓ Challenging tasks → experience↑

4. **Team working**: When production is organized so that groups of workers complete a substantial unit of work – rather than using total specialization where each worker performs one repetitive task. This allows for more empowerment of working people and requires multi-skilled workers.

Advantages: Lower labor turnover
Better ideas → improvement
Consistently higher-quality
For: multi-skilled
more challenging and interesting work
Against: difficult to work closely with others
Strong informal leaders

Quality circles are voluntary groups of workers who meet regularly to discuss work-related problems and issues.

Advantages: quality↑
   Contribution of workers, successful ideas → best solution

Team prize

   5. **Target setting**: Management by Objectives
Purpose: to enable direct feedback to workers on how their performance compares with agreed objectives.

Basic idea: people are more likely to do well when they are working towards a goal that they helped to establish and identify.

   6. **Delegation** The passing of authority down the hierarchy
Empowerment: allowing workers some degree of control over how the task should be undertaken.

C: Evaluation: flexible
Pay and non-pay factors;
Leadership style of management & culture of the organization;

CHAPTER 5
Management Roles and Leadership Styles

Effective management:
Managers are responsible for setting objectives, organizing resources and motivation staff so that the organization's aims are met. Managers' get things done, not by doing all jobs themselves but by working with the through other people.

A: The role of management:
1. Setting objectives and planning
2. Organizing resources to meet the objectives
3. Communicating with and motivating staff
4. Coordinating activities
5. Measuring and controlling performance

B: Leadership:
1. Personal characteristics:
    a) Desire to succeed and natural self confidence
    b) Creativity and encouragement
    c) Multi-talented
    d) Incisive mind

2. Important leadership position:
    a) Directors: senior managers, head of a major functional department;
    b) Managers: an individual responsible for people, resources or decision making;
    c) Supervisors: appointed by management to watch over the work of others; leading a team of people in working towards pre-set goals;
    d) Workers' representatives: elected by workers, either as trade union officials or as representatives on works councils;

3. Leadership or management styles:
    a) **Autocratic** leaders take decisions on their own with no discussion;

armed force and police

- b) **Democratic** managers engage in discussion with workers before taking decisions; full participation in the decision-making process is encouraged.

improve motivation of staff

- c) **Paternalistic** managers will listen, explain issues and consult with the workforce, but will not allow them to take decisions.

Suitable for unskilled, untrained or newly appointed staff, but lead to disappointment and disillusionment in more experience staff;

- d) **Laissez-faire** management: 'let them do it' – allow workers to carry out tasks and take decisions themselves within very broad limits.

Research or design teams;
Disaster: Leaving workers to their own devices with little direction or supervision might lead to a lack of confidence, poor decision and poor motivation

Laissez- faire leadership: A leadership style that leaves much of the running and decision making of the business to the workforce. This may be appropriate in research and development departments staffed by skilled specialists that are self-motivated.

C: McGregor's Theory X and Theory Y:

Theory X and Y: McGregor argued that management attitudes to the workforce vary within two extremes. The views held by management about the workforce will influence both leadership style and managerial decisions.

Theory X is the very negative position in which workers are viewed as lazy, disliking work, avoid responsibility, not creative;
Autocratic management

Theory Y view sees workers as enjoying work, accepting responsibility, creative and willing to take an active part in contributing ideas and solutions

Democratic style

In practice, most managers will have views somewhere between these two extremes.

The structure of Organizations

A: Organizational structure:

Organizational structure is the internal, formal framework of a business that shows the way in which management is linked together and how authority is transmitted.

B: Different types:

1. The hierarchical (or bureaucratic) structure (pyramid):
Advantages: region or country or product category; 'role culture'
Disadvantages: one-way (top downwards) communication
Few horizontal links and lack of coordination between departments
Inflexible → change resistance

2. The matrix structure:
Project team made up of people from all departments or divisions.
Task or project focused
Individual's ability to contribute to the team rather than their position in the hierarchy;
Advantages: Total communication between all members of the tea
The cross over of ideas between people with specialist knowledge in different areas tends to create more successful solutions
Disadvantages: Difficulty of passing down of authority;
Reduced bureaucratic control;
      Conflict of interest of cross-departmental: two leaders

C: Key principles:
1. Levels of hierarchy:
Tall tree: Poor communication, slow messages distorted or 'filtered'
Narrow span of control
Remoteness

2. Chain of command: the route through which authority is passed down on organization – form the Chief Executive and the Board of

Directors.

Orders are passed down; information is sent upwards;

3. **Span of control:** the number of people reporting directly to one manager or supervisor. A 'wide' span of control has many staff reporting to each manager.

4. **Delegation** means the passing down of authority to perform tasks and take decisions from higher to lower levels in the organization.
The wider the span of control, the greater the degree of delegation that is undertaken.

5. **Centralization** means keeping all of the important decision-making powers with head office or the center of the organization.

Decentralization means passing decision-making authority to managers in other areas, departments or divisions, allowing decisions to be taken away form head office.

D: Factors influencing organization structure:
Entrepreneurial structure: small firms → Division of responsibility → Matrix system
1. The style/culture of management
2. Retrenchment ← recession; Competition
Reduce levels of hierarchy and shorten the chain of command.
3. Adopting new technologies: IT

CHAPTER 6

Human Resource Management

Human Resources Management: Modern term for the personnel function which includes a wide range of responsibilities such as recruiting, training and appraising staff in order to increase their efficiency.

Role:
    Manpower planning
    Recruiting and selection staff
    Training, developing and appraising staff
    Developing appropriate pay systems
    Measuring and monitoring staff performance
    Involving all managers in staff development

A: Manpower planning:

Manpower (or workforce) planning: Establishing the workforce needs of the business for the foreseeable future in terms of numbers and skills of employees required.

1. Number of staff:
    a)   Demand for the firm's product:
Influenced by market and external condition, seasonal factors, competitors' actions; trends in consumer tastes;
Temporary or part-time staff with flexible hours' contracts
    b)   Productivity levels of staff:
    Efficient machines → productivity↑ → labor↓ Objectives of the business
    Expend or customer service↑ → labor↑
    c)   Law regarding workers' rights
    Shorter maximum working & minimum wage level
    d)   The predicted labor turnover and absenteeism rate

2. The skills of the staff required:
    a)   The pace of technological change
    b)   The need for flexible or multi-skilled staff as businesses try to avoid excessive specialization

3. Workforce planning – full or part time, temporary or permanent?

Part-time employment contracts:
Advantages:
Firm:
- Overhead cost↓ flexibility, competitive advantages
- Absenteeism↓
- Test of efficiency

Worker:
- Students, parents or elders
- Variety and experience

Disadvantages:
Firm:
- More staff to manage
- Difficulty in communication
- Difficulty in motivation and team work

Worker:
- Earn less
- Low paid rate
- Inferior security and condition
- Low job security

The flexible employment system gives firms the chance to create a small team of full-time staff, called **core workers,** who have full time contract and/ or permanent contract, and combine this with a number of **Peripheral workers** with temporary contract, part time contract or self employed outsiders.

Outsourcing: use of outside contractors to perform specific jobs within the business rather than employing staff directly.

Recruiting and selection staff:
Recruitment process:
   a) To establish the precise nature of **job vacancy** and draw up a **job description (specification)**

Job description: Contains details of a job such as tasks and responsibilities. Used in job advertisements. Often part of the contract of employment.

Job specification: A detail list of the personal skills and characteristics needed from a suitable applicant for a particular job. job title; tasks; responsibility; working conditions; job assessment;
   b) To draw up a **person specification**
   c) To devise a **job advertisement** reflecting the requirements of job and personal qualities

All countries outlaw unfair selection on the basis of race, gender or religion.

2. Selection:
   a) A short list of applicants is drawn up from the application on a CV (curriculum vitae)

   a) Interviews
   b) Other tests (aptitude tests and psychometric tests)

Training, developing and appraising staff:
1. Types of training:
   a) Induction training: all new recruits
   b) On-the-job training
   c) Off-the-job training: outside body (university, computer manufacturer)

2. **Appraising:**
   a) Training can be expensive;
   b) Development and appraisal of staff should be a continuous process;
   c) Appraisal is often undertaken annually;

Developing appropriate pay systems:
Job evaluation is an objective process of identifying the different skills, levels of physical effort, responsibilities and qualifications needed to perform each job effectively.

Measuring and monitoring staff performance:
1. Indicator:
Measuring workforce performance:

a) **labor productivity** = $\dfrac{\text{Output per time period (year)}}{\text{Average number of workers employed in time period}}$

b) **absenteeism rates** = $\dfrac{\text{No. of staff absent} \times 100}{\text{Total no. of staff}}$

c) **labor turnover** = $\dfrac{\text{No. fo staff leaving in 1 yr} \times 100}{\text{Average no. of staff employed}}$

   Internal problems: shortage of staff
           Help to reduce redundancy
   External factors: low rates of unemployment locally
           Better transport

d) Other measures: waste levels; reject rates; consumer complaints

2. Employee performance – methods to improve it:
   a) Appraisal
   b) Training
   c) Quality circles
   d) Cell production and autonomous work groups

e) Financial incentives

F: Involving all managers in staff development:
Other tasks for HR:
1. Contracts of employment for all staff
2. Discipline and dismissal of employees

Dismissal is the act of terminating a contract of employment due to incompetence or indiscipline.

Unfair dismissal: Dismissal of staff that does not follow agreed procedures. Employees may take the issue to an industrial tribunal if they consider their dismissal to be unfair.

Procedure: inability to do the job in situations where necessary and sufficient training

continuous negative attitude at work
continuous disregard of required health and safety procedures
deliberate destruction of an employer's property
continued harassment of other employees

Breach of employment law:
Pregnancy
Discrimination
Being a member of union
Non-relevant criminal record

3. Informing staff of redundancies

Redundancy occurs when the contract of employment is ended by the employer because there is no longer sufficient work for the worker to do, perhaps because of a fall in demand or a change in technology.

Retrenchment to save on costs
Budget cuts
'Last in, first out'

4. Employee welfare: financial support when in need, showing the caring attitude of the business towards its workforce.

CHAPTER 7

Introduction to Operations Management Decisions

Operations management (production management): *is concerned with the* management of resources – land, labor and capital - to achieve efficient output of goods or services that will satisfy the demands identified by the market research department.
- Efficiency of production
- Quality
- Flexibility

A: The production process:
1. Factors influencing value added:

Value added: The difference between the cost of bought – in components and the price charged for the finished products. Value added is not the same as profit – from value added must be subtracted wages, finance costs and overheads to arrive at profit.

    Design of product
    Efficiency
    Promotional strategy

2. **Value analysis**: An analysis of the main features of a product to see if the same performance and style can be achieved at lower cost without reducing its consumer appeal.
   - Performance
   - Appearance
   - Economy of manufacture

Compromise: they will work closely with all relevant departments – marketing, production and finance in particular – to arrive at the best combination of these 3 features.

B: Production, productivity and efficiency:

labor productivity = $\dfrac{\text{Total output in a given time period}}{\text{Quantity of labor employed}}$ = Output per worker

Capital productivity = <u>Total output in a given time period</u> =
Output per capital
Quantity or value of capital employed

1. Raising productivity levels:
    a) Improve the training of staff to raise skill levels
    b) Purchase more technologically advanced equipment
    c) Improve employee motivation
    d) More efficient management

2. Is raising productivity always the answer?
Product; unit cost; wage↑; Unemployment

C: Production methods:
1. Job production:
The production of single, one-off products;
Large and unique products as dam and tunnel;
Individual products as wedding cakes and made-to-measure suits;
New, small firms; labor-intensive;

2. **Batch production:** involves the production of products in separate batches; every item in the batch is completed at each stage before they all pass on to the next stage of production.
Division of labor; economies of scale;

3. **Mass production**: Large-scale production of similar or identical items. First pioneered by Henry Ford, his production systems for car manufacture led to substantial productivity improvements at the cost of no product variation.

4. **Flow production**: The manufacture of a product using a continuous production line. Each stage of production is linked by a continuously moving conveyor belt. The individual products move from stage to stage of the production process as soon as they are ready, without having to wait for any other products.

Usages: Large quantities of output
High and consistent demand
Standardization items

Demand: Careful planning f production process
Advantage: Low labor cost
Constant output rate
Minimization of input stock: just-in-time (JIT) stock control
High and constant quality
Disadvantage: High initial set-up cost
Boring, de-motivating and repetitive job

5. **Mass customization**: This process combines mass production with multi-skilled labor forces to use production lines to make a range of varied products.

Focused or differentiated marketing can be used which allows for higher added value.

Dell computers can make a customized computer to suit your specific needs in a matter of hours. By changing just a few of the key components – but keeping the rest the same, low unit costs and maintained with greater product choice.

6. **Cell production** (cellular production): is the form of flow production, which is separated into a number of self-contained mini-production units (cells). The production line is split into a number of self-contained cells or units.

The cell system has led to significant improvements in worker commitment and motivation and this, in turn, has led to significant increases in productivity. Success depends on a well- trained, multi-skilled work force.

D: Location decisions:
1. Impact: fixed costs: land price
Variable cost: wage rates; transport costs of raw materials
Revenue: service industry
2. Quantitative factors:
    - Site costs
    - Regional incentives: financial support (short-term)

- ✧ Transport costs
- ✧ labor costs
- ✧ Revenue generation

3. Qualitative factors:
   - ✧ Local infrastructure: transport and communication links
   - ✧ Environmental and planning considerations
   - ✧ Management preferences: school, sports and shopping facilities; airport
   - ✧ Clustering: 'Silicon Valley' the same industry locating in the same region

4. Others:
   a) The pull of the market: Internet
   b) Planning restrictions:

Local authorities: employment VS environment

   c) Decision: break-even analysis; investment appraisal
   d) International location – globalization
      - ✧ Exchange rate risks
      - ✧ Trade barriers
      - ✧ Ethical consideration
      - ✧ Political, legal and language considerations

CHAPTER 8

Costs, Break-Even and Costing Methods

A: Costs of production:
1. **Direct costs** are costs that are attributable to (can be allocated to) a particular cost center.
e.g. a product or process. labor & materials
2. **Indirect costs** are the costs which must be covered before the firm makes profit but which cannot be directly attributed or allocated to a specific cost centre.
e.g. Overheads

B: costs → output:
1. **Fixed costs**: fixed, in short run, do not vary with output, such as rent of premises;
2. **Variable costs**: vary directly with output such as raw materials and piece rate labor.
3. **Semi-variable costs**: Costs that vary with output but not indirect proportion, e.g. electricity or telephone costs or salesperson's fixed basic wage + commission;
4. **Marginal costs**: The additional variable cost of producing one more unit of output.

C. Problems in classifying costs:

D. Break-even analysis:
1. The graphical method – Break-even chart is a line graph which shows the firm's break-even point by the intersection of total revenue and total cost lines.

Break-even point is the level of sales at which total revenue is equal to total costs. The firm makes neither a loss nor a profit at this level of sales.

2. **Margin of safety** is the amount by which sales exceed the break-even point. It is an indication of how much sales could fall without the firm falling into loss.

3. The bread-even equation: Fixed costs; Contribution per unit

4. Further uses: A marketing decision
An operations management decision
Choosing between two locations for a new factory

E: Evaluation:
The assumption that costs and revenues are always expressed in straight lines is unrealistic;

Not all costs can be conveniently classified into fixed and variable costs;

There is no allowance made for stock levels on the break-even chart;

It is unlikely that fixed costs will remain unchanged at different output levels up to maximum capacity

Improving operational efficiency:
Capacity, scale of operation and work study

A: Capacity utilization:

$$\frac{\text{Current output}}{\text{Maximum capacity}} \times 100$$

Maximum capacity is the total level of output that a business can achieve in a certain time period.

1. Capacity utilization – impact on average fixed costs

When utilization is at a high rate, average fixed costs will be spread out over a large number of units – units fixed costs will be relatively low.

Advantages of high capacity: Utilization↑ → fixed costs↓ → profits↑

Employees: security & pride
Drawbacks of full capacity: Pressure on staff
Customers will wait for order or turn to competitors
Machinery reliability↓ ← maintenance and repairs↓

2. Excess capacity – what are the options?

Excess capacity exists when the current levels of demand are less than the full capacity output of a business.

a) a short-term, seasonal problem?

Options: 1) Maintain high output levels but add to stocks – expensive and risky if sales do not recover

—

2) Adopt a more flexible production system allowing other goods to be made

   c) a long-term problem resulting from a fashion change, technological development of rival products or and economic recession?

Cut production or rationalization

3. Working at full capacity:
a) Sub-contract: quicker
b) Expending production scale: long-time

B: Business expansion:
1. Economies of scale:
   a) Purchasing economies (bulk buying):
'B2B' (business to business)
   b) Technical economies
flow production lines; advanced technical equipment
   c) Financial economies
- Banks and lending institutions show preference for lending to a big business with proven track record and a diversified range of products;
- Raising finance by 'going public' or by further issues of shares for public limited companies is very expensive, so the average cost of raising the finance will be lower for larger firms selling many millions of dollars' worth of shares;

   d) Marketing economies

The marketing costs can be spread over a higher level of sales for a big firm.

Managerial economies

The skill of specialist managers and the chance of them making fewer mistakes because of their training is a potential economy for larger organization.

2. Diseconomies of scale: Factors that lead to increasing average costs of production when a firm increases its scale of operation. They usually result from the inefficiencies of operating a large organization.

- a) Communication problems:
  - ✧ Poor communication → poor decision
  - ✧ Poor feedback to workers → worker incentive↓
  - ✧ Excessive use of non-personal communication media
  - ✧ Communication overload with the sheer volume of messages being sent
  - ✧ Distortion of messages caused by the long chain of command
- b) Alienation of the workforce
- c) Coordination the business

3. large- scale production – unit costs of production

4. Are diseconomies avoidable?
1. Management by Objectives
2. Decentralization
3. Reduce diversification

C: Work study – improving labor efficiency

1. In its simplest form, work study involves:
- a) Method study: to find the most effective method of undertaking a task
- b) Work measurement: recording output level using different methods and arriving at a

'standard' or target time for each task
2. Techniques:
   a) An improvement in productivity
   b) Improved use of space and equipment
   c) Improved planning as the time for each task would be recorded
   d) The calculation of piece rates for each task
3. Improve on existing work practices:
   a) Select the task to be analyzed
   b) Observe how the task is currently done, noting the flow of materials, movements of workers and the layout of the equipment
   c) Analyze the data gathered
   d) Suggest improvement to the methods
   e) Put the new method into effect
   f) Record the impact of the new method on productivity
4. The key stages in work measurement are:
   a) Decide on the task to be recorded
   b) Record the time taken for the task, making allowances for any necessary stoppages
   c) Rate the performance of the workers against the average performance for workers performing similar tasks
   d) Establish the standard time for the job

5. Common problems:
   a) Workforce resistance
   b) Accurate measurement of tasks

Improving operational efficiency:
Stock management; lean production

Stock: Goods held for manufacture of for sale.
3 main categories: raw materials and components
work-in-progress
finished goods

A: Stock management:
1. Problems resulted from ineffective stock management:
   a) Insufficient stocks to meet unforeseen changes in demand
   b) Out-of-date stocks ← if appropriate stock rotation system is not used
   c) Stock wastage ← mishandling or incorrect storage conditions
   d) High stock levels → excessive storage costs and a high opportunity cost for the capital tied up
   e) Poor management of the stock purchasing → late deliveries, low discount from suppliers or too large a delivery for the warehouse

2. Stockholding costs:
   Opportunity cost
   Storage costs
   Risk of wastage and obsolescence

3. Costs of holding inadequate stocks:
'stock-out' costs – low stock
   a) Lost sales
   b) Idle production resources
   c) Special orders could be expensive
   d) Small order quantities

B: Optimum order size:
The purchasing manager must ensure that supplies of

the right quality are delivered at the right time in sufficient quantities to allow smooth and unbroken production.

Economic order quantity (EOQ): The optimum or least cost quantity of stock to reorder, taking both delivery costs and stock holding costs into consideration.

C: Controlling stock levels – a graphical approach:
- a) Buffer stock: Minimum stocks if a delay in delivery occur or production rates increase.
- b) Maximum stock level: limited by space or the financial costs of holding
  EOQ + buffer stock
- c) Re-order quantity
- d) Lead time: normal time taken between ordering new stocks and their delivery
- e) Re-order stock level: level of stocks that will trigger a new order to be sent to the supplier

D: Just-in-time (JIT) stock control:
Just in Time: Part of the lean production principle. The aim is to avoid holding any stocks – either of materials or finished goods. This requires supplies to arrive just at the time they are needed and products to be finished just as they are sold or dispatched to customers.

1. Requirement:
   - a) Excellent relationships with suppliers
   - b) Production staff must be multi-skilled and prepared to change jobs at short time
   - c) Flexible equipment and machinery
   - d) Accurate demand forecasts
   - e) The latest IT equipment
   - f) Excellent employee-employer relationships
   - g) Quality

2. JIT evaluation:

E: Lean production:
Lean production: The term used to describe the whole concept of trying to manage the production process more efficiently with the minimum of resources. The objective is to eliminate waste of resources and time from original stock ordering through to final customer service.

1. Simultaneous engineering:
Simultaneous engineering: The organization of the stages in product development so that many of them may be undertaken at the same time. This process speeds up the development and launch of new products, possibly allowing a competitive advantage to be gained.

A method of developing new product by ensuring that essential design, market research, costing and engineering tasks are done at the same time as each other – not in sequence or one after the other.

Advantage: early launch of new products

2. Flexible specialisms:
Flexible specialization: Adapting flow production techniques to allow for small production runs of specialist products that meet niche, not mass, market needs.
   a) Flexible employment contracts
   b) Flexible and adaptable machinery
   c) Flexible and multi-skilled workers

Benefits: quicker response to consumer demand changes

3. Just-in-time stock control principle

F: Kaizen – continuous improvement:

Kaizen: The concept of continuous improvement in production processes – rather than one-off leaps forward in productivity.

1. Conditions:
   - ➢ Management culture: involving staff and giving their views and ideas importance;
   - ➢ Team working: suggesting and discussing new ideas to improve quality or productivity is best done in groups;
   - ➢ Empowerment: by giving each kaizen group the power to take decisions regarding work place improvements, this will allow speedier introduction of new ideas and motivate staff to come up with even more ideas;
   - ➢ All staff should be involved

2. Evaluation:
   - a) Radical and expensive solution
   - b) Resistance from senior managers
   - c) Costs
   - d) The most important advances tend to be make early

Chapter 9

**Improving operational efficiency:
Quality issues; Operational Planning**

A: Defining quality:
Importance: a) customer loyalty
b) costs of complaints↓
c) longer life cycles
d) less advertising
e) higher price

B: Quality control technique:
1) Prevention: design
2) Inspection: "zero-defect" manufacturing
3) Correction and improvement

C: Inspecting for quality:
1. Weaknesses:
   1) Looking for problems → culture↓ & resentment among workers
   2) Tedious job → inspector motivation↓
   3) Long time checking
   4) Responsibility: worker → inspector

D: Quality assurance:
Quality control: The process of checking the quality standards of work done or the quality of materials and components bought by the business.

Quality assurance is setting and agreeing those standards throughout the organization and making sure that they are complied with so that customer satisfaction is achieved.
 ✦ Product design
 ✦ Quality of inputs
 ✦ Production quality
 ✦ Delivery systems
 ✦ Customer service including after sales service

ISO 9000: Staff training and appraisal methods

Methods for checking on suppliers
Quality standards
Procedures for dealing with defective products and quality failures
After-sales service

CHAPTER 10

Business Accounting and Finance

A: Importance:
- Start-up capital: cash injections to set up a business
- Working capital: the day-to-day finance
- Further finance for expansion
- Finance for take-over
- Special situations: Sales↓ ← economic recession
- Failure in payment by a large customer
- R&D

B: Capital and revenue expenditure:
Capital expenditure: purchase of assets (long-term, building and machinery)
Revenue expenditure: spending on all other costs and assets (short-term, wages, salaries and materials for stock)

C: Working capital:
Working capital is the net current assets of a business; the day-to-day needed for operating a business, such as the payment of wages and buying of stock.
Current asset − current liabilities
Current assets: stocks; debtors; cash in the bank; tills
Current liabilities: overdrafts; creditors

1. How much?
Opportunity cost; 'working capital cycle'

2. Managing:
a) Debtors
1) Not extending credit to customers;
2) Selling debts to specialist financial institutions;
3) By being careful to discover whether new

customers a creditworthy;
4) By offering a discount to clients who pay promptly;
b) Credit
1) Increasing the range of goods and services bought on credit;
2) Extend the period of time taken to pay;
c) Stock:
1) Keeping smaller stock balance;
2) Using computer systems to record sales and stock level, and ordering as required;

3) Efficient stock control;
4) Just-in-time stock ordering;

d) Cash:
1) Cash-flow forecast;
2) Wise use or investment of excess cash;
3) Planning for too little cash and provision for overdraft facilities made with the bank.

D: Resources of finance:
1. Internal sources:
   a) Profits retained
   b) Sales of assets
   c) Reductions in working capital

2. External sources:
Short-term:
- Bank overdrafts
- Trade credit
- Debt **factoring** is the selling of debts to a debt factor in exchange for immediate liquidity. This releases capital tied up in debts for use in the business. The firm will not sell the debts for 100% of their value – the band acting as the debt factor will offer between 80% and 90% of their value.

Medium-term:
- Hire purchase and leasing
- Medium-term bank loan

Long-term:
- Long-term loans from banks
- **Debentures:** Loan certificates sold by a business to raise loan capital. They usually pay a fixed rate of interest, sometimes secured against a specified asset.
- Sales of shares – equity finance
- Grants: central government
- Venture capital: small business can gain long-term investment funds from venture capitalists

Advantages: of debt finance:
- Ownership
- Loans will be repaid eventually, no permanent increase in the liabilities of the business
- Lenders: no voting rights at annual general meeting
- Interest → corporation tax↓
- Higher return

Advantages: of equity finance:
- Permanent capital not to be repaid
- Dividends do not have to be paid every year

E: Finance for unincorporated businesses:
Sole traders and partnership:
Saving and profit
Bank overdrafts, loans and credit from supplier
Borrow from family and friends

F: Raising external finance – plan:
1. **Introduction**: nature of business, aim and objectives, amount of finance and specific use
2. **A business description**: past performance, legal structure, capital structure, background and business experience of main personnel
3. **Market research and marketing plan**

4. **An operations plan**: products and quality
5. **Financial information**: Forecasted cash flow budget, a projected profit and loss account and balance sheet, forecasted break-even analysis

More successful: think twice; more clearly plan

The need for business accounts

A: Usage:
1. Business managers:
    - Measure the performance of business
    - Take decisions
    - Control the operation of each department
    - Set targets or budgets
2. Banks
    - Lend?
    - Overdraft?
    - Continue overdraft or loan?
3. Creditors (suppliers)
    - Secure?
    - Credit risk?
    - Press for payment?
4. Customers
    - Secure?
    - Future supplies?
    - Security for spare parts and service facilities?
5. Government and tax authorities
    - Tax?
    - More job?
    - Bankrupt?
    - Law?
6. Investors (shareholders)
    - Invest?
    - Profitable?
    - Share of profits?
    - Potential growth?

- Potential investors: Other choice?
- Actual investors: sell?

7. Workforce
    - Wages and salaries?
    - Expand or downsize?
    - Job is secure?
    - Profits → Wage increase?
    - Average wage?
8. Local community
    - Profitable? Expansion?
    - Losses? Closure?
    - Involved?

B: Limitations:

1. Missing data:
- Details of sales and profitability of each product
- R&D plans
- Precise future plans for expansion or **Rationalization** (The process of reorganizing resources to increase efficiency. This often leads to redundancies in an attempt to reduce business overheads.)
- Performance of each department
- Impact on environment and local community
- Future budget

2. Accurate?
- **'window dressing' accounts'**: Adopting accounting practices that are not actually illegal to present a firm's accounts in a more favorable way.
- Selling assets (building) at the end of financial year, then leased or rented back
- Reducing the amount of depreciation of fixed assets (machines or vehicles)
- Ignoring 'bad debts'
- Overvalue the stock
- Delay paying bills or incurring expenses

C: Management and financial accounting:

Management accounting: The production and analysis of detailed internal accounting information used to aid management decision making and for planning and control of operations.

Financial accounting is concerned with the production of the final accounts, in accordance with legal requirement, for the benefit of users such as shareholders.

The final accounts of a business

Final accounts are those accounts that sum up the activities and position of the business at the end of a trading period, e.g. financial year.

A: Profit and loss account: The account that records all of a firm's revenues, costs and profits made over a specific trading period.

a) Trading account:

Gross profit (loss) is the profit make on trading activities before deducting the expenses (overheads) of running the business.

= sales turnover − cost of sales

Sales turnover (Sales revenue): total value of sales made during the trading period

= Quantity sold × price

Cost of sales (cost of goods sold): direct cost of purchasing the goods sold during the financial year.

= opening stocks + purchases − closing stocks

b) Profit and loss sector:
- ◇ **Net profit** = Gross profit − overhead expenses
- ◇ **Profit after tax** = Profit before tax − corporation tax
- ◇ **Overhead:** Business costs that cannot be directly apportioned to one cost centre and that are not generated by a specific production process, e.g. office costs and property rent, management salaries, lighting costs and depreciation.

◇ **Operating or net profit = sales turnover — (cost of sales + overheads)**

Operating or net profit = Gross profit less expenses and overheads before tax and interest.

◇ **Tax:**

c) Appropriation account is the final section of the profit and loss account showing how the profits after tax are distributed between the owners:

=Retained profits + dividend

Dividend is the share of the net profit paid to shareholders. Preference shares usually carry a fixed dividend and ordinary shares a variable dividend dependant on the profitability of the company.

Sales turnover
—cost of sales = Gross profit
— overhead expenses = Net profit
— tax
— dividend
= Retained profits

2. Uses:
- ◇ Measure the performance
- ◇ Compare with the expected profit level
- ◇ Banks and creditors: lend?
- ◇ Prospective investors: invest?

B: The balance sheet: An accounting statement that values, at one point in time, an organization's assets and liabilities.

2. Definitions:

a) Fixed assets are the business assets whose purpose and nature do not change over time. They are recorded at historical cost and depreciated (or occasionally appreciated in value) as and when considered necessary. Premises, vehicles and machinery are examples.

- **Tangible assets:**
- **Intangible assets:** Those assets that have no physical form but which are of monetary value to the business, e.g. patents; trademarks; copyrights; goodwill.

b) **Current assets** are the short-term assets that are likely to be converted into cash before the next balance sheet date. They include bank accounts, stocks and debtors.

c) **Current liabilities** are debts that are likely to have to be repaid within a year.
Trade credits, band overdraft, unpaid dividends and tax;

d) **Net current assets** (working capital) = Current assets − current liabilities

e) **Share capital and reserves (shareholders' fund):** The value of the total investment made by ordinary and preference shareholders.

f) **Capital employed** is the total long-term and permanent capital of the business comprising loans, share capital and reserves.

g) **Assets employed:** fixed asset + current assets − current liabilities

h) **Long-term liabilities:**

C: Cash flow statement:
Cash flow (liquidity): The movement of cash into (income and capital injections) and out of (purchases and expenses) a business.

D: other information:
1. The Chairman's Statement
2. The Chief Executive's Report
3. The Auditor's Report
4. Notes to the accounts

E: Capital and revenue expenditure:
Capital expenditure: Spending on fixed assets that will last for more

than one year and that can be used repeatedly — contrasting with revenue expenditure.

Revenue expenditure: Expenditure incurred to meet day-to-day expenses of the business. It does not add to asset values but pays for incurred costs.

F: Depreciation of assets
- Assets decline in value: normal wear and tear through usage
- Technological change

Straight-line method of depreciation: equal amount of depreciation to profits each year.

<u>Historic cost — residual value</u>
   Expected useful life

Residual value: The expected resale value of a fixed asset once it has reached the end of its useful life.

Analysis of published accounts
Ratio analysis:
- Liquidity ratios
- Profitability ratios
- Efficiency ratios
- Shareholder ratios
- Gearing ratios

A: Profitability ratios
1. Gross profit margin = $\dfrac{\text{Gross profit}}{\text{Sales turnover}} \times 100$
2. Net profit margin = $\dfrac{\text{Net profit}}{\text{Sales turnover}} \times 100$
3. Return on capital employed = $\dfrac{\text{Net profit}}{\text{Capital employed}} \times 100$

B: Liquidity ratios

Liquidity: The ability of a business to meet short-term liabilities (debts).
Liquid assets: Assets that are either cash or closets to it – bank deposits and debtors.

1. Current ratio = __Current assets__
   Current liabilities
2. Acid test ratio = __Liquid assets__
   Current liabilities
   Liquid assets = current assets − stocks

Measures to improve the liquidity: increase cash in, decrease cash out
Sale of redundant assets, canceling capital spending plans, share issue, or getting long-term loans

Investment appraisal

Investment means purchasing capital goods – such as equipment, vehicles and new building – and improving existing fixed assets.
Investment appraisal is the general term for assessing the value of investment projects. The four techniques – payback, average rate, net present value and internal rate of return – are used to determine whether a particular project should be undertaken.

Information needed:
- Initial cost
- Estimated life expectancy
- Residual value
- Forecasted net returns or net cash flows

4 quantitative methods:
- Payback period
- Average rate of return
- Net present value
- Internal rate of return

A: Forecasting cash flows:
= forecasted cash inflow (annual revenue)
− forecasted cash outflows (annual operating costs)

Cash flow forecast: A detailed forecast or budget of a firm's future monthly cash inflows and outflows. The closing monthly balance will indicate either a positive or negative cash position. If negative, the additional sources of finance, such as an overdraft, may need to be arranged.

Negative cash flow: When the value of cash outflows over a time period exceed the value of cash inflows.

B: Quantitative techniques of investment appraisal:

1. Payback method: A method of investment appraisal that calculates the length of time taken to pay back the original investment from a project's net cash flows.

$$\text{Month of payback} = \frac{\text{additional cash inflow needed}}{\text{Annual cash flow}} \times 12$$

a) Reasons:
1) Compare the projects
2) interests ← borrowed finance
3) opportunity cost of other purpose ← internal finance
4) risk ← longer pay back period
5) 'risk averse': reduce the risk to minimum
6) Cash value↓ ← inflation

b) Advantages:
   a) Quick and easy to calculate
   b) Easily understood
   c) The emphasis on speed of return of cash flows → more accurate short-term forecasts of the project's profitability
   d) Eliminate projects of too long payback period
   e) Liquidity

c) Disadvantages:
   1) Do not measure the overall profitability of a project; ignore

　　　　　all cash flows after the payback period
　　2) Concentration on short-term project
　　3) Ignore the timing of cash flows during the payback period

2. Average rate of return (ARR)

ARR = <u>average annual profit</u>
　Initial capital cost

a) Reasons:
　　1) Compare the projects
　　2) Criterion rate (minimum expected return set by the business)

b) Advantages:
　　1) Uses all of the cash flows
　　2) Focuses on profitability
　　3) Easily understood and easy to compare
　　4) The result can be quickly assessed

c) Disadvantages:
　　1) Ignore the timing of cash flows
　　2) All cash inflows are included, the later cash flows are less accurate
　　3) The time value of money is ignored

3. Qualitative factors – investment decisions are not just about profit

　　a) 　　　Environment and local community
　　b) 　　　Risk: local planning official and pressure group
　　c) 　　　And aims and objectives of the business
　　d) 　　　Different managers: different degrees of risk

Cash flow management and budgeting

A: 'The relationship between profit and cash:
Problems: 1. selling↑ → output on credit↑ → danger of short of cash or liquid funds
2. capital expenditure → cash payment on first year

B: Managing cash flow:
1. Cash in
2. Cash out
3. Financial resources? to cover cash shortage

C: Cash-flow forecast: benefits to business
Business: Estimates of cash receipts and payments over the coming months
Anticipated 'cash in hand' or cash deficit
Predicated overdraft
Bank: assess the financial needs, cash flow and liquidity of businesses

D: Dealing with cash-flow problems:
1. Reducing or delaying expenditure
2. Obtain cheaper supplies of materials and components
3. Rent or lease equipment rather than buying it outright
4. Delay the payment of bills – extending the credit period
5. Get cash in more quickly from the sale of goods
    cash on time
    debtor period↓
    sell debts

    BBank **Overdraft:** A bank grants a business the right to borrow up to an agreed amount as and when the finance is required. This is more flexible than fixed term loans.

    short-term loan
    sell assets

About the author: Keith G Parker is the CEO and Business Director for Executive Training Solutions (ETS). He has an extensive background in business management as well as teaching business to non-native speakers to help them enhance the cross-cultural daily business communications that go on around the world. This book is designed for the entry level student into business and offers basic ideas and concepts behind business. This tool is designed to be a guide or supplement to high school or university business and international business majors. All information has been obtained using various avenues and research as well as his own knowledge in teaching business at Shanghai University.

www.ingramcontent.com/pod-product-compliance
Lightning Source LLC
Chambersburg PA
CBHW022022170526
45157CB00003B/1316